Accidents of Being

Poems from a Philadelphia Neighborhood

Accidents of Being

Poems from a Philadelphia Neighborhood

by

Mary Rohrer-Dann

© 2023 Mary Rohrer-Dann. All rights reserved.
This material may not be reproduced in any form, published,
reprinted, recorded, performed, broadcast,
rewritten or redistributed without
the explicit permission of Mary Rohrer-Dann.
All such actions are strictly prohibited by law.

Cover design by Shay Culligan
Cover image, "Sledders at Burholme Park" by Rob Lawlor
Author photo by Michael Dann
Library of Congress Control Number: 2023936118

ISBN: 978-1-63980-326-2

Kelsay Books
502 South 1040 East, A-119
American Fork, Utah 84003
Kelsaybooks.com

For Michael, Chelsea, Anderson, and Elyse Amalie;
my sisters and brother, their spouses and children; and my parents.
And for all whose unheralded lives contain so much quiet courage,
so much loveliness.

Acknowledgments

So much gratitude to Cynthia Mazzant, whose dramatic vision expanded my vision and moved these poems from unpublished page to stage. Thanks to Rob Lawlor, for his painting, "Sledders at Burholme Park," which graces the cover. I am grateful, too, to Marty Lammon, Mary McGuire, Judy McKelvey, Carol Motta, Josephine Pirrone, Sarah Russell, and Virginia Smith for their astute and generous readings of this manuscript. Finally, many thanks to the editors of the following publications where these poems first appeared, sometimes in slightly different form or under a different title.

Boston Literary Magazine: "That Summer"
Comstock Review: "Tante Klara never visited the doctor" (as "Bertha Adler never visited the doctor")
Centered: "Evening Concert," "Riding the 26 Bus with Hermes"
The Drabble: "That Year"
Fifty Words: "When Brendan Tierney Cannot Sleep" (as "Nights He Couldn't Sleep")
Keystone: Contemporary Poets on Pennsylvania (forthcoming): "Before He Fell, or Jumped"
Panoply: "The Stables on Solly Avenue"
Philadelphia Stories: "Uncle Karl Was a Bulls-Eye for Trouble"
Poetry in a Time of Pandemic: "90th Birthday Wish"
Rat's Ass Review: "Land of Reinvention," "Retaining Wall"
Red Eft Review: "Goodbye to All That"
Ruby: "Saturdays," "Filling"
Six Sentence Society: "Spark"
Third Wednesday: "Hannelore Schmidt Comments on Her Neighbor's News" (as "Easter Rabbits"), "Uncle Davy's Near-Regulars," "Liliana Reyes' Days"
Vita Brevis: "Tightrope Pas de Deux"

Author's Note

Burholme Park in northeast Philadelphia and its woodlands, fields, and museum, were my childhood's extended backyard. The potent hold of that landscape, and of the working and middle-class people I grew up among, led to this book of poems. In the tradition of fiction, it is a palimpsest of imagination, experience, and stories I heard directly or as whispers on the air.

Three opening characters are historical. Burholme mansion and its 85 acres were given "Free to the people of Philadelphia, forever" by the estate's heir, Robert Waln Ryerss. Mary Ann Reed, Ryerss' widow and executor (and former housekeeper) traveled worldwide to further furnish his museum. Here, she also becomes an occasional spirit guide.

My characters are primarily European immigrants or of that heritage. While some nearby communities are now much more diverse, my immediate childhood neighborhood is still mostly white and only slowly changing. Continued segregation is a deliberate and troubling fact of American life. However, Burholme Park, as it was created to do, has always drawn a wider group of people who visit its museum and library, play ball there, hold church and school picnics, enjoy the sledding hill in winter. And so, I also give voice to some Black and Latine characters, offered with respect, and I hope, with empathy and accuracy. My aim for all my characters—and for my readers—is appreciative curiosity, emotional integrity, and always, the profound pleasures of story.

Contents

Prologue

Sledding at Burholme Park   17

1860–1916

Summer Retreat   21
Anne Waln Ryerss Saves Another Horse   22
The Horticulturalist Speaks of His Parents   23
Mary Ann Reed Recalls Her First Husband   24

Interlude

Mary Ann Reed Ryerss Baun Contemplates the Afterlife   29

1930–1963

Needs Must   33
That Year   34
Hannelore Schmidt Comments on Her Neighbor's News   35
That Summer   36
The Thrifty Store for Thrifty People   37
Land of Reinvention   38

1961–1980

Girls and Boys   41
The Wild King   42
Retaining Wall   43
American History 1   45
Spark   46
8th grade Social Studies at Jardel Rec Pool   47
Saturdays   49
American History 2   50

The Stables on Solly Avenue	51
American History 3	52
Before He Fell, or Jumped	53
House of Secrets	55
Lillian Robideaux' Great-Niece from Atlanta Arranges the Funeral	56
Faith Presbyterian Picnic at Burholme Park	57
Equinox Rendezvous	58
Freedom Run	59

Interlude

Pet Cemetery	63

1981–2000

Uncle Karl was a Bull's-Eye for Trouble	67
When Brendan Tierney cannot sleep	68
Filling	69
Gift of the Magi	70
Dolly Hofnagle Dreams of the New Pastor	72
Tante Klara never visited the doctor	74
Goodbye to All That	75
Maggie McClean Remembers Her Tierney Aunts	76
Uncle Davy's Near-Regulars	77
Ralph Hauptmeier Walks His Dog Pete	79
Evening Concert at the Park	80

2001–2022

American History 4	83
Shelly Faro Discusses Neighborhood Changes with Maggie McClean	84
Skinny Dipping Under an Orange Moon	85

Ninja Bliss	86
Ruby Morrison Watches Barack Obama's First Inauguration from the TV room at Philadelphia Protestant Home	87
Liliana Reyes' Days	88
Hard Frost, Late April	89
Tightrope Pas de Deux at Burholme Park	90
90th Birthday Wish	91
Riding the 26 Bus with Hermes	92
I Kept My Promise	93
Sledding at Burholme Park: Reprise	94

Prologue

the mere sense of living is joy enough
—Emily Dickinson

Sledding at Burholme Park

Snow days, Saturdays, Sundays after church,
  after school afternoons
    we're zooming down Burholme Park hill
      on waxed cardboard flats
        greased trashcan lids
          rickety toboggans strung with bells

We come from all over: Burholme, Lawndale,
  Lawncrest, Olney, Frankford, Kensington
    in galoshes or buckled boots
      felted wool coats
        slippery snow suits

Mom says, *Don't come back till dinner*
  Dad says, *Listen for my whistle*
    MomMom says, *Meet me when the church bells ring*
      PopPop says, *I used to sled here*

So we fly swerve hurtle careen crash roll
  see how many kids we can pile on one sled
    how many sleds we can link in a train
      how fast how far we can go.

1860–1916

Let me make the songs for the people
—Frances Ellen Watkins Harper, "Songs for the People"

Summer Retreat
(Joseph Waln Ryerss)

Burholme, my splendid pink villa, crowns
eighty-five acres of fragrant woodland,

offers respite from Market Street's stink and clamor.
Anne, still in riding dress, beckons me

with mint tea to the shaded veranda
where our pup Fanny, like a slim white deer,

rises from her rug, trots to my side.
I kiss my wife, smooth my dog's velvet ears,

close my eyes and let fall away the rising
discord with our southern brethren.

At Burholme, I put aside worry of war, hear
only the brook wandering the wood beyond.

---

* Joseph Waln Ryerss, wealthy importer, collector, and Tioga Railroad Co. President, built Burholme, in northeast Philadelphia County in 1859.

Anne Waln Ryerss Saves Another Horse

When the blue roan who earns your bread
stumbles to his knees, you raise your whip
higher, beat him bloody.

Sir, where is the sense in that?

The gelding's teeth tell me he is just
past his fifth year, yet the bearing rein
has already bent his spine.

I appeal to your good judgement.
He needs rest or he will soon be fit
for slaughter only and of no use to you.

Let me take him to my farm to recover.
He will join others from these city streets,
stand to his flanks in rye and fescue.

* Anne Waln Ryerss brought many ill-treated horses to Burholme. Her work continues at *The Ryerss Farm for Aged Equines* in Pottstown, PA, the oldest nonprofit horse sanctuary in the US.

The Horticulturalist Speaks of His Parents
(Joseph Morrison)

Mama and Papa never spoke names known
only to each other, theirs or the place they fled,
a place where they held title to nothing.
Not even their own breath. And if war came,

they had no faith its end would be in their favor.
They rode the trackless train of night river crossings,
of burrowing deep in wagons loaded with soiled hay
or summer squash, trudge of their own rag-bound feet.

Mama's belly bigger each day with me, they forgot
Canada, found safe employ in Philadelphia
with a white man who ran a different kind of railroad,
moved us to his summer home far from watchful eyes.

Two little rooms behind the spring house.

Under my folks' skilled hands, everything
green grew. Now, Mr. Robert heads the estate,
builds new greenhouses. We supply the finest
geraniums for the finest houses in the city.

Mama and Papa passed within a year
of each other, stayed hard-working, shy,
proud into their last days. And wary.
They lived forty years in freedom

but trusted fully no law, nor any white man,
no matter how kindly, no matter slavery ended.
They never spoke their secret names.
They never spoke of any home but here.

* A photo caption of two unidentified Black men states Burholme supplied prize geraniums to Philadelphia estates. A rumor claims that Burholme may have served as an Underground Railroad station.

Mary Ann Reed Recalls Her First Husband

Never, in my twenty-seven years of service,
did he lay a hand on me but in kindness
or instruction, his fingertips cool, dry, giving
me an ebony carving, a glazed ceramic to study.

Trained in law, he devoted himself first
and last to Burholme, his 11,000 books,
collections from foreign travels,
the welfare of his beloved animals.

We found, despite differences in station,
an affinity of like minds. He schooled
my eye to appreciate, my wit
to discern Beauty, History, Value.

Why the crane netsuke is more precious
than the nesting dove, the copper
Laughing Buddha finer than
the ebony *Dancing Shiva*.

His health worsening, he said, "Mary,
your fortitude, courage, and kindred
soul will see my vision through."
He suggested we marry.

He saw a legacy beyond family bloodline:
a free public library, museum of treasures,
leafy woodlands and sunlit meadows for all.
Why would I not honor his trust?

Too ill to venture downstairs, he pledged
himself in the sunny upstairs library.
A thimbleful of champagne, a courtly kiss.
I helped him to his solitary bed.

* Mary Ann Reed, Ryerss housekeeper for 27 years, married the heir, Robert Waln Ryerss in 1885, shortly before his death, shocking family and society. She upheld her promise to fulfill his wishes to bequeath the estate "Free to the people of Philadelphia, forever."

Interlude

Each is before, and each behind its time.
—Djuna Barnes, "Pastoral"

Mary Ann Reed Ryerss Baun Contemplates the Afterlife

How have I come to *be* again?
Suddenly, I *am*.
Then, *not*.

Abruptly, I am walking
rooms once intimate,
now rearranged.

Or watching from the cupola
children in strange dress ride
the snowy hill or roll down lush grass.

How have I come to *be* again?
Suddenly, I *am*.
Then, *not*.

Sometimes, a scent of horses,
or geranium, drifts on the air, or
the noisy reek of a mowing machine.

Time's kaleidoscope shifts
but always
I am tethered here.

I never stroll Robert's beloved Beirut,
or visit the wards of the Asylum
I built there in his name.

I never sit with John on our porch
at Linley, the home we built
and cherished for ten years.

I am grateful not to return to that hot
Peking room, my lungs filling with glass,
John's gentle touch too much to bear.

Still. What is this accident of being
that brings me always, only, here?
Alone?

---

* In 1899, Mary Ann married Rev. John Baun after fifteen years as executor and sole collector for Robert's estate. They traveled widely, continuing to purchase artifacts and treasures for the museum until her death in Peking in 1916.

1930–1963

The world begins at a kitchen table.
—Joy Harjo, "Perhaps the World Ends Here"

Needs Must

Brendan Tierney does what needs must
so his Ma and sisters don't go hungry,
seven of them in two drafty rooms
over O'Malley's on the Avenue.

A bone-thin boy, smart, strong, stubborn,
his nimble fingers sift trash for what
he can peddle. Or pick a pocket or two
when food's scarce and rent's due.

Been running numbers for Mack McKenzie
since his Da left for God knows where
after the hosiery mill let him go.
A year on the bread line, then gone.

Hard on a man to watch his littles starve.

But Brendan never poor-mouths his Da,
fights till he's bloody anyone who does.
And his Ma? She takes in sewing
but pisses holy water, to hear him talk.

Brendan will be a fierce fine thing if ever
he gets some meat on his bones. Dark curls,
eyes blue as the Holy Mother's cloak.
Girlies lookin' his way and he's but fourteen.

That Year
(Kathleen Byrne)

She walked to school alone,
cut through a weedy lot
searching for clues.
In the weedy grasses,
a dented stop sign
bright as a wound
shattered bricks
chunks of asphalt
a gauzy blue scarf
netted with cobwebs
and what drew her
over and over
the burnt burlap sack
from which a moldering cat
fur charred black
struggled forever to escape,
teeth and sprung claws
like long yellow pearls.

Fall passed.
Then winter.
Her mother dying.
Dead.

Hannelore Schmidt Comments on Her Neighbor's News

Hanne! Emil Vogel bellows from his porch.
Ich habe zwei Osterhasen! Jungen!
Easter Rabbits, he gloats. Boys.

Thumps his chest like Johnny Weissmuller, struts
inside, where he's surely eating the onion cake
I brought yesterday, toasting himself with schnapps.

Past sixty and still at it. *Hund!*

Poor Corinna, deep in her forties and laboring
long into this Easter morning scented with rain.
Six *Kinder,* and now two more to pull at her.

People here think I couldn't catch a man.
Ha. I caught a man.
Then I caught a baby.

I walked alone to the root woman. Snarl
of black hair, red scarf. Demanded Geld
before she let me in, then brewed a bitter tea.

Afterwards, she washed me so tenderly, I wept.

I left the whispers behind. Made my own way,
my own life. I own my house and everything in it.
No man tells me what to do or how to do it.

I boil coffee on my new enamel stove, gather
my needles and wool, begin a second blanket
here on this rain-washed American street, where
shameless old men shout their news for all to hear.

That Summer

Ralph Hauptmeier found himself in deep woods
igniting rotted fence posts, yellowed newspaper
with gasoline siphoned from his father's truck.

He longed to confess to Father Mathias, but
how to speak his body's constant conflagration,
its luscious buzz in the sizzle-suck of air?

One afternoon behind the shed, his fingers
closed on a matchbook in his pocket.
It was flame before he knew it, flame

vaulting as he watched, struck, flame
lighting the thick fuse of Virginia creeper
that climbed the house where his mother

lay in the back bedroom napping,
the new baby curled at her breast.
From afar, he watched himself grab

the hose coiled in the shed, attach
mouth to faucet, his hands steady.
No one ever knew.

His sister grew, a slow, sunny child
with eyes bright as green glass.
She would never marry, never leave home.

He knew this had nothing to do with him.
He knew it had everything to do with him.

The Thrifty Store for Thrifty People
(Kathleen Byrne)

At this hour, it's easy to find
seats on the El and trolley home.
On my feet from noon to nine,
a dollar a day in Ladies Bargain Coats
at Snellenburg's downtown. I'm beat.

But there's that dark-haired, blue-eyed,
skinny young man sitting across from
me again. He says a shy *hello*
then flashes a grin that tells me
he's not shy at all.

I take a chance, let him sit next to me.
Brendan, he says. His eyes are so
blue! I tell him my name and he
asks if I'd like an egg cream at
the Quaker Diner by Five Points.

Aunt Bridget won't worry if I'm late.
Sometimes I get a late supper
at Horn & Hardarts after work.
So, I grin right back (I'm not shy, either!)
say, *Yes*.

Land of Reinvention

1.

Roland Robideaux was colored
in Gainesville and Atlanta,
Creole in Terrebonne Parish.
In the City of Brotherly Love,
Black neighbors find dog shit
on their front stoop, so when he
and Lillian buy a new house
on a new street near Burholme Park,
he becomes white.

2.

Lillian Robideaux claims
she is the fourth Gabor sister.
Who's to say she is not?
On this street of aproned hausfraus,
thick-ankled babushkas, she cooks
in gold toreador pants,
twinkly, high-heeled sandals.

1961–1980

And what did I see I had not seen before?
Only a question less or a question more;
Nothing to match the flight of wild birds.
—Edna St. Vincent Millay, "Wild Swans"

Girls and Boys
(Lucy Faro)

Girls can TOO be Daniel Boone! I scream at my brother and run run run to Burholme Park and up the sledding hill and past the swings to the woods and the creek where everything is green and shadowy and still and I slip past spiders in their webs and sleepy moths and the animals think I am one of them and I find two eagle feathers striped blue and black and I don't need my brother's fake coonskin hat, I am Mingo, and I hear a branch snap and I freeze, listen for the outlaws who kidnapped Daniel Boone's family, and I creep across the log swaying high above the rapids and I am armed with just my tomahawk and my courage but Daniel Boone is counting on me.

The Wild King
(Gina Capelli)

Summer afternoons, Burholme Park
is a golden prairie, the sledding hill
a ridge where I guard my herd against
horse traders who want to break us,
fit us with steel bits.

I am not a girl.
I am a wild black stallion.
The mares and foals depend on me.
They graze in high yellow grass,
toss their manes in rising wind.

Far off, a bird cries. Thunderheads loom.
I prick my ears.
The warning sounds again.
I charge down the hill, round up the herd,
gallop home as Dad whistles *dinner* one last time.

Retaining Wall

Another miscarriage. Another failure.
Scooped, like fruit rotted from the inside,
Lillian Robideaux stares at the backyard

retaining wall, its blank reproach.
Silk debris of spent mimosa blossoms
drop into her lap. Perhaps she will lie

in this chaise forever. But Roland's Pontiac
rumbles down the drive. She swivels Revlon's *Hot
Coral* across her lips, opens her silver compact.

It slips, shatters. Slash of blue sky, shards
of green eye, pink cheek, her sunflower hair,
glare up at her. A jay screams from the wall.

Later, curled into Roland, she pretends
to sleep. He kisses her hair, whispers,
We can try again, Lil.

He will never tell her no,
will hush her worry that this
is one more price for their love.

How many more times before they are both in pieces?

After Roland leaves for work, she gathers
old cement mix from the garage, leftover
bathroom tiles, empty liquor bottles.

From the kitchen junk drawer, a frayed Spanish
fan, orphan buttons, loose string of her First
Communion pearls, tiny as baby teeth.

Each morning, she takes bits of brokenness
and makes the concrete wall a breathing thing.
Knobbed lid of a chipped teapot becomes

a nippled breast. Cracked plate, a cobalt face.
She fashions ovaries from mother-of-pearl
earrings, from a wrecked rose dish

makes a winged, light-filled uterus.

American History 1
(Lucy Faro)

Mrs. Quigg, sobbing, opens our door.
Miss Gatter hurries into the hall.
No one shoots a spitball or falls
from their chair, not even Henry Cash.
Miss Gatter returns.
"Our President has been shot.
Go straight home."

Gina and I run outside.
The early afternoon light,
the empty trees,
the intersection without
Mrs. Brill, our crossing guard,
our dazed faces—
nothing is familiar.

Spark
(Ingrid Hauptmeier)

The lumber yard's on fire, Dad shouts. *Let's go!* Mom's at choir practice, so me and Abby pile into the Galaxy and roar down the street, Dad's two-way radio screeching, night air surging with sirens, smoke, blasting horns, ash. We swerve behind the Acme, park at the far lot overlooking the train tracks, inch down the steep ravine and across the tracks. The world swirls black and orange, churning with flying cinders, frantic birds, cracking trees, the boom of superheated air. When Mom finds out—it will be bad. She'll never let this go. But every bit of my body is awake! I clutch Dad's hand and Abby's, breathe through the wet kerchief he tied around my mouth, tremble before a gushing waterfall of flame.

8th grade Social Studies at Jardel Rec Pool
(Lucy, Gina, Ingrid)

1.

We sit in cramped countries of crabgrass and concrete.
Gold Stars of David, silver crosses, or crucifixes strung
on chains around our necks signify new allegiances.

We court the lifeguard's mirrored gaze, anoint each
other with baby oil, comb *Sun-In* through our hair,
shudder away wasps and rumors. We croon to Motown
on our transistors, the only Black voices we know.

2.

We might sit on the pool edge while the lifeguards
pour buckets of chlorine, even kick like crazy with
the little kids to disperse it, but we no longer dive
like dolphins between each other's legs.

Only lezzies do that.

We shun the dank locker room, the bodies there:
mothers with swollen bellies, thick triangles of dark hair,
old women with chicken-skin thighs, terrible breasts.

3.

We confess that our nipples stiffen in cool water;
agree only sluts use tampons. Of rough fingers
expert at pinching tender breasts, slipping
inside bikini bottoms, we cannot speak.

Once, we would have kicked—hard!—where it hurts.
Now, we wonder: should we feel special? Chosen?
We macramé friendship bracelets to stave off loneliness.

4.

Ask us what violence is and we'll name high school boys
who swing bike chains after Saturday night dances,
or that green, distant T.V. country burning nightly,

or (though we are told they have nothing to do
with us) those American cities burning—
even ours, mere miles away.

For the shop teacher who sucker-punches delicate
boys awkward with calipers and circular saws,
for all the ways we are learning to separate,
segregate, isolate—ourselves from each other,

ourselves from our selves—we have no words yet.

Saturdays
(Vogel children)

His twelve-hour, six-day week hoisting crates
   of powdered eggs, fifty-pound sacks of flour,
     blocks of butter, mixing batter in huge tubs,
       rolling out pie crusts, braiding stollen, grating
         hazelnuts, slicing apples, lifting laden
      pans into giant ovens, retrieving them
    bright with heat and yeasty fragrance, beating
confectioner's sugar and cream, piping
   faultless pink roses, precise green leaves—
     our father, his twelve-hour, six-day week over,
       his Pall Mall breath leavened with Schmidt's,
         set on our kitchen table the white box
       filled with all that hadn't sold that day:
    cinnamon buns enameled with molasses,
  doughnuts oozing blackberry jam,
sweet cheese and blueberry Danish,
   and butter cake, crisped froth of butter and sugar.

This labor. These offerings.

American History 2
(Lucy Faro)

The morning after
Dr. King is assassinated.
Third period, Social Studies.
Mr. Braverman calls roll.
He pauses.
Says Chet Johnson's name. Tenderly.
Everyone turns, stares at Chet's empty seat.

The Stables on Solly Avenue
(Gina Capelli)

The warm shadows, the dusty light—Holy.
The smell of horses, their flesh,
   their manure, the sweet hay—Grace.
Their soft nickering to one another—Song.

She gives chunks of apple to the horses
who lift their heads to greet her,
strokes their whiskered muzzles, calls
the names of the shy or cautious.

And her favorite, Greek, a gentle,
fine-boned bay gelding. In the purple
depths of his eyes, she finds a solace
she does not know how to ask for.

She grieves her body, newly strange, urgent.
She grieves her home, its silences, sudden shouts.
And her faith, its desertion deepening until,
at Easter, she yearned for grace. And felt nothing.

Here, in the nimbus of dust motes,
the snuffling and shuffling of beautiful creatures,
she feels revealed to herself, again known
to what she once would have called God.

American History 3
(Lucy Faro)

Hot sun.
Hushed crowd.
Gina
and I
wait.
Someone
calls to us.
Mrs. Karp
Mr. Braverman
Miss Renfroe
cross the tracks
circle us in their arms.
Slow, awful rumble.
Bobby's Kennedy's funeral train.

Before He Fell, or Jumped

Before he fell, or jumped, Robby Krawic,
wayward altar boy in black jeans, battered
high tops, Marlboros snug against his bicep,
was going places no Septa bus could take him.

Before he jumped, or fell, Robby Krawic
at Jardel Rec dances made Jagger look tame,
made girls cant their hips when he turned
his dark-eyed slouch their way.

Before he jumped, or fell, Robby Krawic
drove Patty home from her special school
days their mother worked, let her crank
the radio, shout the words to "Satisfaction."

Before he fell, or jumped, Robby Krawic
wore a gold Saint Jude medal palmed
from St. William's parish store, sold
smokes lifted from Kresge's.

Before he jumped, or fell, Robby Krawic
could hotwire any car, beat any souped-up
Mustang or Firebird in his gold Barracuda,
Friday nights down Decatur Road.

Before he fell, or jumped, Robby Krawic
in his Steve McQueen shades sauntered
through neighborhood parties at the park.
Fathers frowned, mothers touched their lips.

Before he jumped, or fell, Robby Krawic
sat with a six-pack on his pitched roof.
Something happened to his sister Patty
when he forgot to pick her up from school.

After he fell, or jumped, Robby Krawic
never danced, only hobbled, watched
from his basement room the girls forget him,
guys from school leave for Nam or Canada,

the world spin on without him.

House of Secrets

No one had seen the Robideaux in a while,
their drapes closed, no bin out on trash day.
Lucy Faro's dad called the police

who found them in their bed, satin duvet
tucked to withered chins, candlewax pooled
on the dresser, needle ragging the turntable.

Roland wore an indigo robe.
Lillian, a yellow kimono splashed with poppies.
Their heads tilted towards each other.

One last secret.

Piles of old *Playboys* and *Photoplays,*
poker decks, valium vials, dusty high heels,
unpaid hospital bills, stacks of LP's—

Monk, Miles, Bird, Billie, Nina, Peggy Lee.
And in a worn wallet, a photo of three boys,
two dark-skinned, one light.

*Sc*ribbled on the back:
Booker, Rex, and Roland, 1932.

Lillian Robideaux' Great-Niece from Atlanta Arranges the Funeral

Back in the sixties, Great-Aunt Lillian
and her Roland chose a simple plaque.
The young Black saleswoman urges an upgrade.

*Wouldn't it be nice to remember your loved ones
with an engraved stone or monument?*
She opens a thick binder to fancier options.

Except for a blurry photo of a little lip-sticked
girl posing in gaping high-heels, Gran's baby
sister vanished early from family stories.

She run off and we never heard from her again.

But when Gran died, Mom found letters:
jubilant, defiant, pleading, bitter. Letters
on pale yellow paper. Unanswered.

The young woman brings out another sample book.
I do not mention the clause in the old burial deed:
Interment for persons of the White race only.

Bile filled my mouth when I read that.
Rohit is Brown.
Our boys are Brown.

Lillian and Roland never had children.
Were they afraid to?
Was this burial plot a way to give

the finger to a world that denied them?
For years, no one in the family cared
to know anything about them.

Let them keep their secrets.

Faith Presbyterian Picnic at Burholme Park
(Rev. Charles Davis)

Feels good, this cool green after gritty
city heat. Marcus, the younger Morrison boy,
brings me a lemonade, some of his mother's
peach cobbler. He points up at the mansion,
asks, was it part of the Underground Railroad.

I shrug. *Don't know. But my great, great,*
great-auntie Henrietta Duterte did run a station.
Owned a funeral home on Lombard Street,
disguised folks fleeing slavery as mourners.
They walked in procession right out of town.
Some people she even hid in coffins.

Marcus goes still, his gaze turns inward.
He's got a hungry mind, and deep,
but keeps his own counsel.
He's going places.

---

* Henrietta S. Bowers Duterte (1817–1903), first female undertaker in the US, was an abolitionist and agent for the Underground Railroad.

Equinox Rendezvous

A weirdly warm December night.
Lucy hunches on the back stoop.
Everything inside her is smashed.

Her parents won't look at each other.
Her brother, back from 'Nam, won't look at her.
The boy she loves no longer loves her.

Wind rises, shadows shapeshift. Fairy lights
flicker from the vacant house next door.
A whiff of *Shalimar,* cigar smoke, brisk

smell of gin. Tenor sax and cymbal washes.
A throaty giggle. Through the hedge, younger
than she ever knew them, Lucy watches

the Robideaux dance. Lillian sways in gold
heels, swirly black dress, beauty mark winking
at her lavish mouth. Roland taps his cigar,

twirls and dips and swings her, their
pinky rings flashing like shooting stars.

Lucy looks up at a confounding sky.

The Robideaux are seven months dead.
The boy she loves loves someone else.
Anything can happen.

Freedom Run
(Marcus Morrison)

After Thanksgiving grace, Jesse announces
he's leaving next week for Fort Dix.
Daddy slams the table. The dishes jump.
They gonna ship you right straight to 'Nam.
You know how many neighbor boys we already lost?
Jess says, *You look at these streets lately?*

Momma's eyes are cold fire, *I won't let you.*
Jesse says softly, *I'm of age, Momma.*
Already signed.

Daddy swears, turns to me. *Don't you be*
getting ideas, Marcus. Four years fighting
Hitler and that GI Bill did jack-shit for me.
Couldn't get a mortgage for a decent house,
locked out of plumbing and electric unions,
working two jobs to keep food on this here table.

Momma flicks her eyes from Jesse to me.
Marcus going to graduate and go to Temple.
I'll clean toilets again if I have to.

Daddy and I don't agree on much anymore but
he's right when he says, *You're not cleaning no*
more toilets, Pearlie. Ever. He looks at me hard.
You gonna put that brain of yours to real use,
keep books for your uncle in Camden.

It burns him that Uncle Louis owns his business,
but says he'll treat me fair. He wants us all to stay
close to home, bring some money in like Ella does.
She graduated five years ago. Still sharing
a room with the little ones. Still got a curfew.

I got ideas. I got plans. I'm going to college,
like Momma wants. But not to Temple.
I been working with Mr. Graham in Guidance
to make sure I graduate with honors. Wants
me to try for the Mayor's scholarship to Penn.

But I'm done with Daddy telling me what to do,
done with these streets, this bullshit city
of brotherly love, where Julian Greely
from Math Club walked straight into gang
fire coming home from the SAT's.

I'm planning on a full ride to Howard in D.C.
Gonna study *our* history, *my* history.
Making my own freedom run.

* Thomas Edison High, a largely Black all-boys school in North Philadelphia, lost more graduates (64) in the Vietnam War than any other high school in the country.

Interlude

A firefly flitted by
"Look!" I almost said
But I was alone
   —Taigi

Pet Cemetery
(Mary Ann Reed Ryerss Baun)

after Donald Hall

By the west veranda
beneath the slender elm
a circle of small white stones.

I long for a brief visit,
a small, fleeting presence
a flickering familiar weight

against my knee, a glimpse
of brown or white or speckled fur,
warm huff of equine breath.

Oh, Fido, Fanny, Brown Dog, Ponto, Little Nelly,
Old Grey.

1981–2000

*What did I know, what did I know
of love's austere and lonely offices?*
—Robert Hayden, "Those Winter Sundays"

Uncle Karl was a Bull's-Eye for Trouble
(Vogel Children)

Stones, fists, curb-hopping cars, schemers
and scammers inevitably found him.
He fell on rocks, plummeted from trees,

stumbled on sidewalks studded with glass.
Once, at City Course, a renegade ball
at the thirteenth hole knocked him cold.

A cheeky mama's boy who never left home,
a good bar fight, a bad bet, he excelled
at upping the ante. And losing.

At family parties, he taught us to chug
orange soda to his whiskey shots, smash
our Ritz crackers in raucous toasts.

Christmas Eve afternoon, he'd light
a smoke, crack a beer, time us as we fired
tinsel missiles at Grandmom's tree.

When she died, he stood dazed at our door,
his heart beneath booze-splotched skin
already swerving towards its dead-end skid.

Five years later, prescription overdue,
he collapsed outside Rite Aid
on Rising Sun Avenue. Bluff called.

During his wake, we imagine him
sitting up in one last prank, giving
us all the finger, his old cock-eyed grin.

When Brendan Tierney cannot sleep

he counts
cats chasing
grasshoppers
across the ceiling.
Some nights,
amber eyes luminous,
one pauses
leaps down
onto his bed.

Tonight
a fine-boned grey
soft and silent
as fog
lands lightly, curls
against his hip
      As did his Kathleen
      for fifty short years.

Filling

Thanksgiving morning, nails bitten to stubs,
Christian's thick fingers mince onions fine as glass
slivers with a small sharp knife, dices celery
in pale green cubes, parsley into deep green flecks.

He pushes all from scarred cutting board
to the deep bowl where hunks of stale bread
soften in warm milk. "Ready, *Schatz*."
He takes a long sip of beer.

Liesel steps from the giblets sauteing in butter,
brings him salt, white pepper, *Maggi,* rubbed sage.
This will be the last Thanksgiving they host.
Time for the kids and grandkids to take over.

Christian takes another sip, rolls up his sleeves,
kneads it all into what the Vogels call "filling."

Gift of the Magi
(Ralph Hauptmeier)

Pete asleep at his feet, twinkle lights
flickering like memory, Ralph ponders
the Dickens Village he and Ellie would
arrange each first Sunday of Advent.

He'd string the lights around the window,
she'd hang the Moravian Star,
position the ceramic houses and shoppes.
After, they had tea with lemon and schnapps.

Christmas Eve, she'd unwrap his gift to her,
another fanciful cottage or figurine, something
she'd bought herself downtown the year before
at Wannamaker's After-Christmas Sale.

She would open the box, revealing
a little mirrored ice rink with rosy skaters,
a tavern to tuck against the steepled church.
Only way to get the sinners to Mass, he'd say.

She always insisted he wrap her gift himself.

They weathered some hard years when
the kids were young; she'd kicked him out,
didn't let him back for what felt forever.

She was right to do it.

Despite the itch, he never chased another fire.
The year she placed a ceramic firehouse
with its red engine beside the bakery
he knew for sure they were good.

Three years now, he fixes the window alone.
Ellie packed Christmas away after Epiphany.
Ralph keeps it long into January, seeking,
still, the promise of the ancient mystery.

Dolly Hofnagle Dreams of the New Pastor

Surfacing from her dream of Pastor Dan,
his bay rum cologne, Dolly wakes to Martin's
sleep-sour breath, forty years of marriage.

Later, she rereads St. Aidan's Bulletin:
*Pastor Dan Invites All to dine
or serve lunch at our soup kitchen.*

Dolly is not a volunteering kind of person.
She minds her own business. But, here
she stands at St. Aidan's door, smells

cabbage, chicken fat, burnt potato
coiling round her. She turns away.
Remembers the pulse of her dream.

Pastor Dan. She searches Fellowship Hall
where the "guests" dine, guests who look
past her or slit their eyes at her tight smile.

Baptized, confirmed, married at St. Aidan's,
Dolly feels a trespasser. In her own church!
And she's worn her best embroidered apron.

Oh, ye of little faith.

Bay-rum spice skates through body odor and hot
grease. Pastor Dan! Sleeves rolled over muscled
forearms, well-worn jeans gripping his thighs

he hands a platter to a grey-faced man,
jokes with a woman with twitchy eyes,
touches a grimy toddler's cheek.

Nods to Dolly.

After dessert, before the guests shuffle out,
Pastor Dan sits at the old upright. Everyone sings.
Praise God from whom all blessings flow!

Tante Klara never visited the doctor
(Lucy Faro)

without making him a marble cake high as a top hat,
or noodles, wide and yolk yellow, cut on a board
scored by decades of noodles, decades of mourning:
no children and a husband dead too soon.

Mein Alfred, she'd whisper, her brown eyes bitter
as apricot pits, her thin arms knotted from chopping,
stirring, kneading, weeding, pushing the ancient mower,
scrubbing the week's grime from the front steps.

Saturday afternoons, I'd help unpin her hip-length
hair, wash it in the sink. Later, she'd reheat
the last of last Sunday's roast for our supper,
dress greens with vinegar sharp as flame.

When my heart shattered, she ladled egg-drop
soup into two green bowls, spoke of her own
heartbreak at seventeen. That I'd endure,
someday find a truer love. I did.

Eighty-five, furious at her heart's stammer
against the steep lawn, the sheets of noodles
rolled paper-thin, she demanded the doctor fix it.
I watched him eye the lopsided cake, yield.

The surgery gave her ten more years, and voices
whispering in the hall, nights when she woke alone
and cried out, a girl again, calling for her mother
—and no answer but moonlight, an empty chair.

Goodbye to All That
(Gina Capelli-Kaminski)

The house emptied, she lies on the floor
of her parents' bedroom, the ancient fan
pushing air thick with heat and shadow.

They argued throughout her childhood,
voices muddy behind the door, except
for the hurled curse—*Puttana! Stronzo!*

Did they make her under this creaking fan?
And was she made in joy, or mere animal need,
as she and Ben had made their youngest,

lying afterwards in silence, bodies subsiding,
hearts raw, both counting the minutes until
he returned to the guest room down the hall.

Her parents seemed to find their way back.
Did they have more faith in love,
in each other? Or was it simply

the Old World dictum against divorce?
And at what cost? Tomorrow
she will sit with her widowed father

at closing and pass the house to its new
owners, a Latino couple, first on the block,
the tiny woman's belly big with twins.

Maggie McClean Remembers Her Tierney Aunts

Bridget and Nora never married,
never moved far from their childhood home,
lived lives larger than their married sisters.

Bridget ran Rising Sun Tax Services.
Nora took photos for Otto's Ads.
Both embroidered altar cloths for St. Williams.

Bridget, the pretty one, was stiff-necked and stern.
Nora had buck teeth, wide blue eyes.
The family pondered their spinsterhood,

suspected Nora's sunburst smile hid a broken heart.
Never imagined proud Bridget kept letters in
a red lacquer box from a boy killed at Luzon.

Bridget loved Shakespeare, Becket, Ionesco.
Nora knew 300 birds by song, silhouette,
flight pattern: raptors were her specialty.

They traveled separately and together:
Sistine Chapel, Las Ramblas, Hagia Sophia,
the Great Wall, the Winter Palace, Marrakech.

Retiring in their seventies, they sold the house,
moved to separate retirement homes.
We wondered: had they a falling out?

Bridget died a week after seeing Derek Jacobi
in Uncle Vanya. Nora tucked the lacquer box
into her coffin with a book of poems by Rilke.

Then she traveled the Amazon, sending us postcards
noting what she'd seen: harpy eagles, horned screamers,
masked trogons, king vultures, cocks-of-the-rock.

Uncle Davy's Near-Regulars
(Ingrid Hauptmeier-Jensen)

I unwrap the Christmas present
Hank picked up at Uncle Davy's
cramped rowhouse in South Philly.

Hank snorts at the flimsy cardboard box.
Goddamn, he says.
I drove an hour in a blizzard for this?

I laugh—*Hush! It's Christmas—*
open the lid stamped: <u>Deluxe
Chocolates—Near-Regulars</u>.

Loose, misshapen chocolates.
All those dinners you fed him, Hank says.
Those shirts you bought. Cheapskate!

But I remember being twenty and broke,
a year left at Moore College of Art, Mother
saying, *If it's that important,*

ask your rich uncle for help.

I baked a pan of apple dumplings,
made my case in Uncle Davy's parlor
that reeked of cigars, sardines, Brylcreem.

He ate a dumpling. Ate another.
His small eyes glared. *I should
know what I'm funding, yeah?*

I returned with my best work. Charcoal
studies of Oma's hands, an oil of pale pears,
my favorite self-portrait in troubling blues.

I remember him studying each piece,
his thick fingers tipping cigar ash
into an old TV dinner tray.

Those are Gerda's hands.
He pulled out his checkbook.
It's a loan, he said, *not a gift.*

He gave me the check,
then the empty pan, still sticky
with cinnamon and syrup.

I stir Uncle Davy's chocolates,
pop one into my mouth,
give Hank a buttercream kiss.

Ralph Hauptmeier Walks His Dog Pete

You used to just let the dog out.
You didn't *walk* him.

He ate what you ate, gnawed
Friday's soup bone on Saturday.

You kept the doghouse clean and dry.

But here's Ralph following Pete's fat
backside all over town, pockets

stuffed with treats, his arthritic fist
cupping Pete's greying muzzle.

Ellie's gone. Six years in April.
He's had Pete for five.

Sometimes Ralph hears Ellie
as he heaves Pete onto their bed.

Who rescued who? she laughs.

Evening Concert at the Park
(Maggie McClean)

Young families sprawled in the grass
make me ache for when you were small.

Curled on a checkered quilt, a mother
traces letters on her daughter's back

as your Nana Kathleen did for me
so long ago, and I did for you.

How you loved that game—love it still—

luscious touch light as smoke,
nexus of consonant and vowel.

My palm spanned your little-girl shoulders,
narrow blades opening into adolescence.

Now, when you are too briefly home,
we practice the body's calligraphy once more.

How lovely, your shoulders' broad elegance,
How shapely, the strength of your hands.

2001–2022

I will take the sun in my mouth
and leap into the ripe air
      Alive
         with closed
eyes
to dash against darkness
  ——e.e.cummings, "Crepuscule"

American History 4
(Lucy Faro)

We watch the screen in the faculty
lounge after dismissing the kids—
What did we tell them?
What does it mean?
Those two planes
those two towers
gone.

Shelly Faro Discusses Neighborhood Changes with Maggie McClean

First, the Robideaux house, then Capelli's.
Now it's the McNally house going
to Mexicans or Puerto Ricans. Whatever.

My parents came here after the First war, yours, too.
The Hankes and Krawics, after the Second.
They wanted more for their lives, for their kids.

These new people. He's a teacher. She's a cop.
Her mother lives with them. Still, they're not
like us, their dark coloring, talk that makes

you dizzy, backyard parties going all night
and jangly music, their cooking smells
that hurt your throat, make you cough.

Lucy's kids look hard at me—*why do you care,*
Nana, if my best bud wears a hijab?
What will you do if my boyfriend is Black?

What if I'm queer? nonbinary?

I've never heard some of these words.
But what can we do, Maggie?
They're our grandkids.

Skinny Dipping Under an Orange Moon
(Christian Vogel)

Ah, Schatz. Remember how we'd tiptoe
out the creaky back door, the kids and all

the neighborhood asleep, patio stones still
warm against our feet, grass cool where we

dropped our towels, climbed the ladder, slipped
into water that slid like silk across our skin.

We'd float in dreamy suspension, fingertips
touching, just us and a fat orange moon.

I took the pool down years ago.
Each day you slip further beyond my reach.

But whenever I smell sunbaked stone,
hear trees moving in soft night-wind,

I am swimming under that burning moon
with you.

Ninja Bliss
(Shelly Faro)

Men in hard hats pry off
the sewer grate, lower
a huge vacuum hose.

The Reyes boys crouch
on the curb in Ninja Turtle PJs,
faces trembling with light.

Colossal sound floods the street.

Narrow bodies bursting in bliss,
the boys leap into the air,
scream and stomp and boogie.

So good to have little ones
on our block again.

Ruby Morrison Watches Barack Obama's First Inauguration from the TV room at Philadelphia Protestant Home

You know it's only this chair keeping me
from being there in DC's frosty air as Barack
places his hand on the Bible, takes his oath.

I'd be standing tall and proud as Michelle,
his queen in creamy gold, I'd sing with
audacious Aretha in her magnificent hat.

Sally Renfroe with a fresh perm and blue
rinse rolls up in her chair, chirps,
A new day, Ruby. The bigots have lost!

Sally taught high school civics.
She should know better.

But, oh! Those Black and Brown faces
on the dais, in the crowd, every sweet
color there is, shining far as the horizon.

Men, women, babies, teens, grands
and great-grands the world over
weeping, shouting, laughing, dancing.

Today's too glorious to worry foolishness.
Sally, I say, *My grandnephew Marcus—
the one running for District Attorney?*

*He brought me a bottle of champagne.
Dolly's making her so-called famous pound cake.
You bring some cheese and crackers.*

We'll watch the People's Inaugural Ball, toast us all.

Liliana Reyes' Days

Some days, the white-gold
sun steeps in matte-grey cloud

Some days, shadows dapple the white walls
with smoky green and lavender

Some days, a pucker of green tomato
recalls grit of cornmeal, Mami's smoking skillet

Some days, at Reichert's Meats, an old man
pushing his cart behind me, sings *Dos Gardenias*

Some days, desire, that old devil, beats, beats,
beats his wild drum between my legs

Some days, my grandsons' voices dip, lift past
my window, swallows on invisible spools of air

Some days. Oh! Some days.

Hard Frost, Late April
(Lucy Faro)

Earth Day, and my tulips
bend low in grief, their
folded leaves holding
ice crystals huge as rock salt.

The sun climbs blue sky
skimmed with thinning cloud.
The tulips lift their cups,
suggesting, perhaps, a turning.

I know better than to find
signs in blossoms or shining skies.
Still.
Please.

Let me keep trying to nurture that turning.

* On April 20, 2020, former Minneapolis police officer Derek Chauvin was found guilty of murdering George Floyd.

Tightrope Pas de Deux at Burholme Park
(Grace McClean and Leo Gonzalez)

Under two sugar maples

afternoon slowly drifting
into September

we

touch fingers, murmur
encouragement

take turns walking
the trembling line.

90th Birthday Wish
(Tierney-McClean Family)

We zoom in from a dozen households.
Laughing, talking. Our usual family chaos.

Slumped in her wheelchair, Mom sleeps on.
Will she recognize our blurry faces on the tiny screen?

We used to visit weekly. Sometimes, daily.
It's been almost a year.

We sing *Happy Birthday* in clashing
keys and tempos. Her eyes remain closed.

To the aide trying to rouse her.
To our determined cheer.

"Mom," we call. "Happy Birthday, Mom. We love you."
She sleeps on.

Dearest Mama. What good is our love, locked
away by Covid? Alzheimer's?

Here is our wish. May you stay
only until we can visit again.

May your wish to "go home" come true
when we can touch you, hold you, wish you

Godspeed.

Riding the 26 Bus with Hermes

Below ads for JDate, the Barnes Museum,
a Sharpied scrawl: *Black Lives STILL Matter,*
Hermes sprawls on the cracked vinyl seat.

Bobbing to his earbud beat, he is eleven
or twelve, cocoa-skinned, golden-eyed,
braids like lithe serpents twitching beneath

a purple bucket hat strewn with galaxies.
His winged sneakers—iridescent green, gold
foil, flame-orange—crackle and spark.

Velvet-cheeked trickster god, spirit-sprite
of transitions, thieves, travel, and poetry,
what messages do you bring from the immortals?

How will your slight shoulders carry ours to them?

I Kept My Promise
(Mary Ann Reed Ryerss Baun)

Time's kaleidoscope shifts
    and again, children's laughter spangles the air
        a man with a crooked leg pushes his giggling
            sister on the swings
    two sweethearts promise each to the other
on the museum veranda
        an old man sings to his flop-eared mutt
    a sad-eyed woman marvels at ivory carvings
        chanting people wave signs:
            SAVE BURHOLME PARK!
families picnic under the timbered pavilion
    a couple sits in tender silence
        under golden sugar maples
        a young girl turns pages
            in the sunlit library
                imagines worlds
Robert, your dream lives on.

---

* After a 5-year battle, a PA Commonwealth Court ruled that Burholme Park lands remain intact, citing Robert W. Ryerss' will. The adjacent Fox Chase Cancer Center wanted to lease and develop 20 park acres.

Sledding at Burholme Park: Reprise

Snow days, Saturdays, Sundays, after school afternoons,
    we're zooming down Burholme Park hill
        on rocket sleds, sliders,
            snow scooters,
                Retro Flexible Flyers

We come from all over: Cheltenham, Mayfair, Tacony,
    Rockledge, Rhawnhurst, Fox Chase
        in *Minions* parkas,
            light-up fuchsia snow boots
                Brother Shark balaclavas

Mom says, *listen for my text*
    Dad says, *text me when you're done*
        MomMom says, *I used to sled here*
            PopPop says, *how do I text you?*

So we fly swerve hurtle careen crash roll
    see how many kids we can pile on one sled
        how many sleds we can link in a train
        how fast
            how far
                we can go.

About the Author

Philly-born-and-bred, Mary Rohrer-Dann spent many childhood and teenage hours exploring and daydreaming in leafy Burholme Park and its wonderfully quirky museum-library. When visiting Philadelphia family and friends, she makes time to wander the park and museum again, visit the little pet cemetery, and perhaps catch a glimpse of Mary Ann Reed Ryerss' ghost.

An earlier, verse-play adaptation of *Accidents of Being* was produced and staged by Tempest Productions, Inc. in Philadelphia, New York City, and State College. The author's other works include *Taking the Long Way Home* (Kelsay Books, 2021) and *La Scaffetta: Poems from the Foundling Drawer* (Tempest Productions, 2015). She is currently finishing a collection of flash fiction. She makes her home in State College, PA, but will always be a Philly girl at heart.

www.ingramcontent.com/pod-product-compliance
Lightning Source LLC
Chambersburg PA
CBHW071010160426
43193CB00012B/1993